Perspectives

Dangerous Animals
What Do You Need to Know?

Series Consultant: Linda Hoyt

Flying Start
to Literacy®

Contents

Introduction

Is it fair to blame wild animals if they harm us? What is our responsibility?

Animals defend themselves when they feel threatened. They can do this by biting, stinging, scratching, or charging. So if you come across an animal in its natural habitat, you could be in danger. Would you know how to stay safe?

Are so-called dangerous animals all bad? You decide!

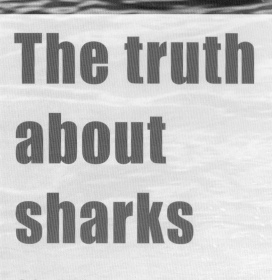

The truth about sharks

Of all the creatures in the sea, none inspire greater fear in swimmers everywhere than sharks!

But how dangerous are sharks to us? Or, are we more dangerous to them?

What do you think?

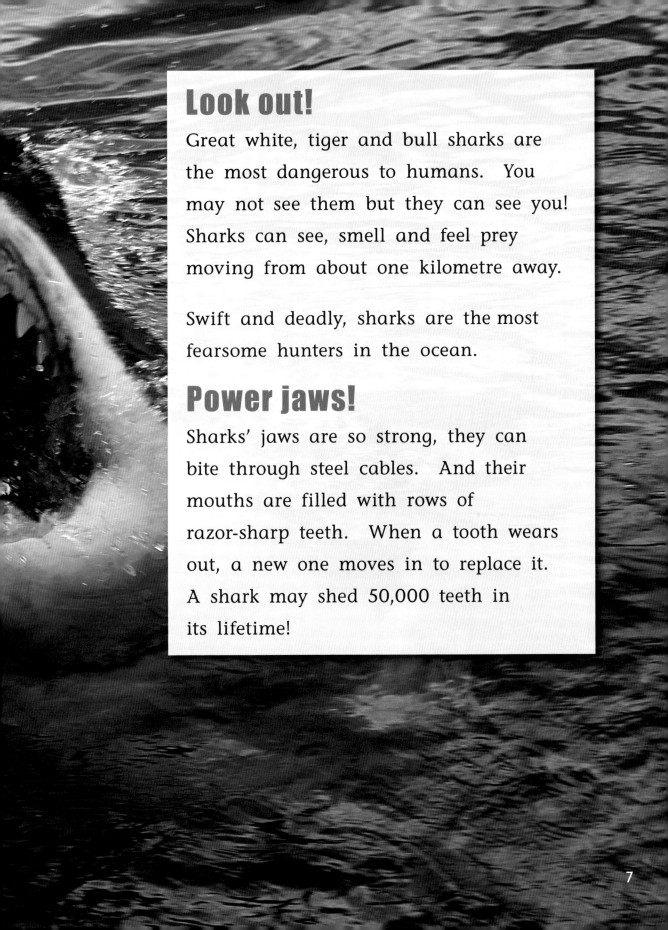

Look out!

Great white, tiger and bull sharks are the most dangerous to humans. You may not see them but they can see you! Sharks can see, smell and feel prey moving from about one kilometre away.

Swift and deadly, sharks are the most fearsome hunters in the ocean.

Power jaws!

Sharks' jaws are so strong, they can bite through steel cables. And their mouths are filled with rows of razor-sharp teeth. When a tooth wears out, a new one moves in to replace it. A shark may shed 50,000 teeth in its lifetime!

Sharks

Of all the creatures in the sea, none are more beautiful or more misunderstood than sharks.

Top predators

Sharks are at the top of the ocean food chain and help keep the oceans healthy. Sharks eat fish, squid and other ocean animals – not people.

Safe to swim

The truth is, sharks avoid humans and rarely bite. On average, one person every year dies from a shark bite in Australia. That makes sharks far less dangerous than cows, which kill about seven Australians a year.

If a shark does bite, usually it's just curious, or has mistaken a surfboard for a seal. Like any wild animals, sharks will bite if you disturb them.

Endangered

Humans kill 100 million sharks every year. Some are hunted for food. Others are caught accidentally in fishing nets. We are far more dangerous to sharks than they are to us!

Speak out!

Are all animals dangerous? Read what these students think.

Some tiny animals are dangerous. Mosquitoes are small but in some places deadly. In some countries around the world, mosquitoes carry disease. So when you are bitten, they can pump the disease into you. This is why you should always check if you need an injection before travelling.

Are lions really dangerous? To me, it depends, because yes, they can kill. But we also kill animals to eat them.

Many animals can be dangerous. Some pets can be dangerous if they are frightened or if you invade their space. My cat can be dangerous. If she doesn't want to do something, she scratches!

Last summer, when I was hiking with my dad, we saw a snake. I was really frightened, but Dad helped me to stay calm. He said we must take care not to frighten it because we were hiking in its home. Dad made sure that we were wearing the right gear before we went hiking. I was wearing long pants and shoes.

I'm not scared of snakes

Written by Jennifer Butchet

Cobra Caroline founded a snake rescue organisation called Reptiles Alive. And her two best friends are snakes!

How would you like to have two snakes as "best friends"?

What do you do as a wildlife rehabilitator?

I'm licensed by the state to nurse injured reptiles. I've looked after snakes that have been hit by cars or lawn mowers, attacked by cats, and tangled in plastic landscape netting. After taking them to the vet, I care for them until they're ready to be released back into the wild.

You also rescue snakes, right?

Yes. At Reptiles Alive, we take in many unwanted snakes that used to be pets.

Are you scared of being bitten?

I use special equipment (gloves, snake hooks) so that I don't come into direct contact with venomous snakes. But snakes are so scared of people that their main goal is to get away.

Do snakes help us?

Yes! They eat tonnes of rodents that eat our crops and spread disease. And their venom is used to make medicine that helps treat people with cancer, heart disease and other ailments. A snake could save your life one day!

Snake aware!

Australia has the most venomous snakes of any country in the world. So if you're hiking in the bush, what should you do to stay safe? What should you do if you see a snake?

Snake safety...

• Wear long pants and heavy shoes.

• Only walk on marked tracks.
Don't walk in long grass off track.

• Pay attention and scan
the track ahead of you.

• If you see a snake on the track,
stay calm and move away to a safe
distance to allow the snake to get away.

• Do not touch or attempt to capture the snake.
This is when most bites occur.

How to write about your opinion

State your opinion

Think about the main question in the introduction on page 4 of this book. What is your opinion?

Research

Look for other information that you need to back up your opinion.

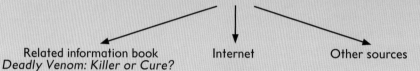

Related information book
Deadly Venom: Killer or Cure?   Internet   Other sources

Make a plan

Introduction

How will you "hook" the reader to get them interested?

Write a sentence that makes your opinion clear.

List reasons to support your opinion.

Support your reason
with examples.

Support your reason
with examples.

Support your reason
with examples.

Conclusion

Write a sentence that makes your opinion clear. Leave your reader with a strong message.

Publish

Publish your writing.

Include some graphics or visual images.